VISUALIZE BELIEVE ACHIEVE

A THIRTY DAY JOURNEY TO LIVE YOUR LIFE WITH A SMILE!

RITA-ANNE FUSS

◆ FriesenPress

Suite 300 - 990 Fort St
Victoria, BC, V8V 3K2
Canada

www.friesenpress.com

Copyright © 2019 by Rita-anne Fuss
First Edition — 2019

For every journal sold $5.00 will go toward the nonprofit - SMILES - Supporting Mental Illness Lives Everyday Society.

For more information or to support SMILES please contact: changingsmiles365@gmail.com

The author can be reached on Facebook - www.facebook.com/rfuss
Instagram - @ritaannef LinkedIn - www.linkedin.com/in/ritafuss

This book is intended to help make informed choices and is provided solely for the user's information with the understanding that the author is not engaged in rendering any professional services. If you seek further help that might require professional treatment please reach out to an expert. Call Crisis Services Canada at 1-833-456-4566 if you are in distress.

All rights reserved.

No part of this publication may be reproduced in any form, or by any means, electronic or mechanical, including photocopying, recording, or any information browsing, storage, or retrieval system, without permission in writing from FriesenPress.

ISBN
978-1-5255-5270-0 (Hardcover)
978-1-5255-5271-7 (Paperback)
978-1-5255-5272-4 (eBook)

1. SELF-HELP, JOURNALING

Distributed to the trade by The Ingram Book Company

This Journal belongs to

_____

INTRODUCTION

Many of us suffer from loneliness anxiety, depression, and the difficulty of coping day to day. I have witnessed it in my family and with friends. Mental illness does not discriminate. The human condition is such that people from all walks of life experience times when they feel that they cannot cope day to day. We might think that they are happy and upbeat, but unless we dig deeper, we may not realize how much suffering is going on inside.

It wasn't until I was an adult that I discovered my father had depression, and not a bad flu that would keep him in bed for weeks at a time. A smart and passionate man, my father became immobilized by depression throughout most of his life. My mother passed away in her early fifties and never shared with me how much he was suffering. Depression was in our family's history, but it remained a secret until, in my late twenties, I made the discovery.

It is okay to feel sad, lonely or anxious sometimes. However, if our emotions become too much to handle we should never feel guilty or be afraid to reach out, even if it's for a hug. We become stronger knowing we are not alone and believing in ourselves doesn't happen overnight. We have to work at it every day.

Throughout my life, I've had struggles with sadness and over time I have grown in confidence to believe in myself and know that *I am enough*. A lifetime of journaling has allowed me to write down my thoughts and feelings, which has proven to be very healing where I can reflect on the blessings in my life and the goodness I possess. These beliefs, practices and my faith have helped me gain a healthy perspective.

This is what inspired me to write this journal. To share some steps that may help you on this thirty-day journey. To provide you with direction, motivation, and action as you capture your thoughts and note what you are grateful for. Writing down an inspirational thought or idea, can change your day to make it more positive. This enhances your mental health and helps brighten your everyday life to face each day with a smile.

During the time of writing this journal, I started a nonprofit society: ☺ *SMILES* ☺ *Support Mental Illness Lives Everyday Society*. For every journal sold five dollars will go towards mentoring, events, conferences and workshops to promote and encourage positive changes. This society and this journal will support and help anyone move toward improved mental health and happiness.

You can **visualize** your day in a positive way, **believe** in yourself, and **achieve** what you set out to do while enjoying the journey. **Believe** it!

DEDICTATION

This book is dedicated to my son Justin, who helps me understand how we each experience sadness differently and to live life each day in the moment.

To my daughter Melody, who lives life to the fullest and helps me, with her kindness and honesty, to be the best mom I can be.

I am so proud of you both, and love you with all my heart.

This book is also dedicated to my loving husband Curtis, who, with unconditional love and support, believes in me and gave me the courage to write this book. I love you forever and ever, amen.

ACKNOWLEDGMENTS

A big shout out to the FRIESENPRESS team for helping me through the publishing process. I also want to give BIG HUGS and a huge THANK YOU to Ruby Berlin, Angela Domet, Denise Kalynchuk, Janell Mayer and Michele Parker for stepping up and joining me in my nonprofit by becoming my first five board members for SMILES. We have a great team for our nonprofit that will Visualize, Believe and Achieve great things to help others!

HOW TO USE THIS JOURNAL

Follow the prompts in the journal by answering the questions in the morning. This will provide a *focus* for the day. In the evening, write down what you are *grateful* for and your *thoughts*. Have an open heart and share your feelings within these pages. Open up to new possibilities and never give up hope.

What do you tell yourself? What ideas do you put into your mind? Sometimes we fail to realize how our thoughts and choices may affect ourselves and others. The way we see ourselves has a great effect on our attitude toward life and how we feel. Keep moving forward, even if that means simply focusing on one small thing a day. We can change our negative beliefs by visualizing something different. Therefore, **visualize** yourself as the beautiful person you are. **Believe** that you are doing the best you can, and you will **achieve** so much more.

Visualize, Believe and Achieve... today!

This journal is intended to help you make informed choices and is provided solely for the user's information with the understanding that the author is not engaged in rendering any professional services. If you are in need of further help that might require professional treatment, please reach out to an expert.

Call Crisis Services Canada at **1-833-456-4566** if you are in distress.

DAY 1

Date: ___ /___ /___

When I am journaling and it's something negative, I will always end with something I am *thankful* for.

What is one thing I can do today when I get out of bed that will make me smile? ☺

☺ My *Thoughts* for the Day ☺

I'm *thankful* for _____

I'm *thankful* for _____

I'm *thankful* for _____

_____

_____

_____

_____

_____

_____

_____

_____

_____

_____

_____

_____

DAY 2

Date: _____ / _____ / _____

I will feel content with what I do today. It's okay if I'm feeling sad. I don't have to be happy all the time. I will be in the moment.

What activities do I like to do? How do I feel when I'm having fun?

_____
_____
_____
_____
_____
_____
_____
_____
_____
_____
_____
_____
_____
_____

☺ My *Thoughts* for the Day ☺

I'm *thankful* for _____

I'm *thankful* for _____

I'm *thankful* for _____

_____
_____
_____
_____
_____
_____
_____
_____
_____
_____
_____
_____

DAY 3

Date: ____ / ____ / ____

When I want to say or think a negative comment, I will turn it into a positive one. Over time, I will change my self-image and see myself as the beautiful person I already am.

What positive words can I tell myself if I'm feeling negative or down?

_____

_____

_____

_____

_____

_____

_____

_____

_____

_____

_____

☺ My *Thoughts* for the Day ☺

I'm *thankful* for _____

I'm *thankful* for _____

I'm *thankful* for _____

DAY 4

Date: ____ /____ /____

Do I self-sabotage? What do I say to myself? I need to tell myself that I am a great and wonderful person. I am beautiful! I am unique! I love myself! I am confident!

What is one thing I will work toward to feel content and confident right now?

_____
_____
_____
_____
_____
_____
_____
_____
_____
_____
_____
_____
_____

☺ My *Thoughts* for the Day ☺

I'm *thankful* for _____

I'm *thankful* for _____

I'm *thankful* for _____

_____

_____

_____

_____

_____

_____

_____

_____

_____

_____

_____

_____

_____

_____

_____

DAY 5

Date: ____ /____ /____

I will look in the mirror and I will give myself a great big smile. I will say out loud "I love myself."

What can I do today that interests me and puts a smile on my face?

_____
_____
_____
_____
_____
_____
_____
_____
_____
_____
_____
_____

☺ My *Thoughts* for the Day ☺

I'm *thankful* for _____

I'm *thankful* for _____

I'm *thankful* for _____

DAY 6

Date: ____ /____ /____

I will accept what I'm feeling and let it go. I will just be in the moment and not try to analyze why I'm feeling the way I am.

What coping strategies can I use today to help me when I feel stressed? Take deep breaths? Go for a walk? Journal?

_____

_____

_____

_____

_____

_____

_____

_____

_____

_____

_____

☺ My *Thoughts* for the Day ☺

I'm *thankful* for _____

I'm *thankful* for _____

I'm *thankful* for _____

_____

_____

_____

_____

_____

_____

_____

_____

_____

_____

_____

_____

_____

DAY 7

Date: ____ / ____ / ____

I will listen to my inner voice encouraging me to take that first step. I am no better or worse than anyone else. I am a loving person.

Write some things I like about myself, and say them out loud.

_____

_____

_____

_____

_____

_____

_____

_____

_____

_____

_____

_____

_____

☺ My *Thoughts* for the Day ☺

I'm *thankful* for _____

I'm *thankful* for _____

I'm *thankful* for _____

DAY 8

Date: ____ /____ /____

I will pray or meditate. We live in a busy world, and I need to take time for myself and have some quiet time. Prayer or meditating will help me achieve that. Pause and take a breath.

How do I feel when I sit quietly for five minutes and slow down to focus on my breathing or prayer?

_____
_____
_____
_____
_____
_____
_____
_____
_____
_____
_____
_____

☺ My *Thoughts* for the Day ☺

I'm *thankful* for _____

I'm *thankful* for _____

I'm *thankful* for _____

_____

_____

_____

_____

_____

_____

_____

_____

_____

_____

_____

_____

_____

_____

DAY 9

Date: ____ / ____ / ____

I believe in myself and visualize myself in the future. I see myself as the amazing person I am. I see myself already where I want to be. It's a commitment. I will work toward being more confident.

How do I feel when I am confident in what I am doing?

☺ My *Thoughts* for the Day ☺

I'm *thankful* for _____

I'm *thankful* for _____

I'm *thankful* for _____

DAY 10

Date: ____ /____ /____

I will establish a daily routine. I need to be organized in what I do and plan my day or week. Even if I accomplish one thing on my list I will check it off and smile. I will feel good about what I did do!

Write a checklist of what I need to do today. I will enjoy the benefits of getting something accomplished in my day.

_____

_____

_____

_____

_____

_____

_____

_____

_____

_____

_____

☺ My *Thoughts* for the Day ☺

I'm *thankful* for _____

I'm *thankful* for _____

I'm *thankful* for _____

_____

_____

_____

_____

_____

_____

_____

_____

_____

_____

_____

_____

DAY 11

Date: ____ /____ /____

I will have a positive attitude. I will have a smile on my face. I will smile at someone today and they will smile back. It feels good.

Where will I likely encounter people today with whom I can share a smile?

☺ My *Thoughts* for the Day ☺

I'm *thankful* for _____

I'm *thankful* for _____

I'm *thankful* for _____

_____

_____

_____

_____

_____

_____

_____

_____

_____

_____

_____

_____

_____

DAY 12

Date: ____ / ____ / ____

I need to take time for myself, and before I start my day do the 5-5-5 rule. Five minutes of prayer or meditation, five minutes of stretching, and five minutes of writing in my journal.

What routine can I start every morning that will help me feel better?

_____
_____
_____
_____
_____
_____
_____
_____
_____
_____
_____

☺ My *Thoughts* for the Day ☺

I'm *thankful* for _____

I'm *thankful* for _____

I'm *thankful* for _____

_____

_____

_____

_____

_____

_____

_____

_____

_____

_____

_____

_____

_____

_____

_____

DAY 13

Date: ___ / ___ / ___

I know that change is good. I will not be afraid of it. I may not like it at first but once I do it, usually it works out for the best, and there was a reason for it to happen in my life.

What is something I need to focus on today that will be good for my soul?

_____

_____

_____

_____

_____

_____

_____

_____

_____

_____

_____

_____

☻ My *Thoughts* for the Day ☻

I'm *thankful* for _____

I'm *thankful* for _____

I'm *thankful* for _____

DAY 14

Date: ___ /___ /___

I will be prepared. The more I prepare, the easier it is. I have a checklist of what I need before I start my happy day.

Write something I've accomplished since I started this journal. I'm proud of what I've done!

_____
_____
_____
_____
_____
_____
_____
_____
_____
_____
_____
_____

☺ My *Thoughts* for the Day ☺

I'm *thankful* for _____

I'm *thankful* for _____

I'm *thankful* for _____

_____
_____
_____
_____
_____
_____
_____
_____
_____
_____
_____

DAY 15

Date: ____ / ____ / ____

I will step out of my comfort zone. I need to be willing to try new things. The more I step out of my comfort zone, the more confident I will become.

What is one thing I can do today that I've never tried before or find difficult to do?

_____

_____

_____

_____

_____

_____

_____

_____

_____

_____

_____

_____

_____

☺ My *Thoughts* for the Day ☺

I'm *thankful* for _____

I'm *thankful* for _____

I'm *thankful* for _____

DAY 16

Date: ____ /____ /____

When someone compliments or recognizes something nice about me, it makes me feel important and good. It makes me react in a positive way.

What do others compliment me on that I am good at?

_____
_____
_____
_____
_____
_____
_____
_____
_____
_____
_____
_____

☺ My *Thoughts* for the Day ☺

I'm *thankful* for _____

I'm *thankful* for _____

I'm *thankful* for _____

DAY 17

Date: ____ / ____ / ____

I will listen more. When I ask questions, I will listen to get to know the other person better. I will pause and think about what I'm going to say before answering.

What is one thing I can do today to help someone else, to put a smile on their face?

_____
_____
_____
_____
_____
_____
_____
_____
_____
_____
_____
_____
_____

☺ My *Thoughts* for the Day ☺

I'm *thankful* for _____

I'm *thankful* for _____

I'm *thankful* for _____

DAY 18

Date: ___ /___ /___

I will call my friends and stay in touch. It's important to follow through and call them back when they call me.

Who am I thinking of right now that I will call today to let them know I was thinking about them?

☺ My *Thoughts* for the Day ☺

I'm *thankful* for _____

I'm *thankful* for _____

I'm *thankful* for _____

DAY 19

Date: ___ /___ /___

I will take the time to do something nice for someone else and notice how it makes me feel. It can become a ripple effect.

How can I be of service to others around me to raise my energy and theirs? A smile? A hug?

☺ My *Thoughts* for the Day ☺

I'm *thankful* for _____

I'm *thankful* for _____

I'm *thankful* for _____

_____

_____

_____

_____

_____

_____

_____

_____

_____

_____

_____

_____

_____

DAY 20

Date: ____ /____ /____

I will focus on breathing deeply—in through my nose and out through my mouth—when I have moments of stress or anxiety. It helps let that moment pass.

In what situation might I practice this breathing technique today to help me feel calm and relaxed?

_____
_____
_____
_____
_____
_____
_____
_____
_____
_____
_____
_____

☺ My *Thoughts* for the Day ☺

I'm *thankful* for _____

I'm *thankful* for _____

I'm *thankful* for _____

_____
_____
_____
_____
_____
_____
_____
_____
_____
_____
_____
_____
_____
_____
_____

DAY 21

Date: ____ / ____ / ____

I have the choice to have a great day or a bad day. I have the choice to be happy or sad. It's up to me. *Smile!*

What positive words can I say to myself to make it a happy day if I'm feeling sad?

_____

_____

_____

_____

_____

_____

_____

_____

_____

_____

_____

_____

☺ My *Thoughts* for the Day ☺

I'm *thankful* for _____

I'm *thankful* for _____

I'm *thankful* for _____

_____

_____

_____

_____

_____

_____

_____

_____

_____

_____

_____

_____

_____

DAY 22

Date: ____ /____ /____

I will be true to myself and work on areas I need help with. I need to stop making excuses. I will be confident that *yes,* I can do it!

What have I started that I need to finish today?

_____
_____
_____
_____
_____
_____
_____
_____
_____
_____
_____
_____

☺ My *Thoughts* for the Day ☺

I'm *thankful* for _____

I'm *thankful* for _____

I'm *thankful* for _____

_____

_____

_____

_____

_____

_____

_____

_____

_____

_____

_____

_____

_____

_____

_____

DAY 23

Date: ____ /____ /____

I will take action. Reading this is one thing, but I need to do something every day and make it happen. I can do it! It's my choice.

What are my unique talents and gifts I can share with others? What am I good at?

☺ My *Thoughts* for the Day ☺

I'm *thankful* for _____

I'm *thankful* for _____

I'm *thankful* for _____

_____

_____

_____

_____

_____

_____

_____

_____

_____

_____

_____

_____

DAY 24

Date: ___ /___ /___

I need to work toward where I want to be. I will start today and choose to take action.

What can I let go of today to clear some space for what I really need to do?

☺ My *Thoughts* for the Day ☺

I'm *thankful* for _____

I'm *thankful* for _____

I'm *thankful* for _____

DAY 25

Date: ____ / ____ / ____

I will be accountable for my actions. I will not blame others. If I look ahead three years from now and I am the same as today, it's because of choices I have made, and I can still change them.

What can I tell my younger self about what I know today?

_____

_____

_____

_____

_____

_____

_____

_____

_____

_____

_____

☺ My *Thoughts* for the Day ☺

I'm *thankful* for _____

I'm *thankful* for _____

I'm *thankful* for _____

_____
_____
_____
_____
_____
_____
_____
_____
_____
_____
_____
_____
_____

DAY 26

Date: ___ / ___ / ___

I will have a plan for my day and follow through. I will take a deep breath and get ready, set, go!

What is something I can get rid of in my home to help with decluttering my mind? What am I holding onto that I will let go of today?

_____

_____

_____

_____

_____

_____

_____

_____

_____

_____

_____

_____

_____

☺ My *Thoughts* for the Day ☺

I'm *thankful* for _____

I'm *thankful* for _____

I'm *thankful* for _____

_____

_____

_____

_____

_____

_____

_____

_____

_____

_____

_____

_____

DAY 27

Date: ____ /____ /____

I will build my confidence. The more I practice at something, the better I get. Over time it will give me confidence, even if I don't think I have it. I will learn to be confident.

What is the first thing that comes to mind that I need to do today that I've been putting off?

_____
_____
_____
_____
_____
_____
_____
_____
_____
_____
_____
_____

☺ My *Thoughts* for the Day ☺

I'm *thankful* for _____

I'm *thankful* for _____

I'm *thankful* for _____

_____

_____

_____

_____

_____

_____

_____

_____

_____

_____

_____

_____

DAY 28

Date: ___ /___ /___

When I feel sad or lonely I can pray or meditate and God will listen. I will take a breath, listen to my heart, and smile.

What is my heart telling me right now when I close my eyes and listen?

_____
_____
_____
_____
_____
_____
_____
_____
_____
_____
_____
_____

☺ My *Thoughts* for the Day ☺

I'm *thankful* for _____

I'm *thankful* for _____

I'm *thankful* for _____

_____

_____

_____

_____

_____

_____

_____

_____

_____

_____

_____

_____

DAY 29

Date: ____ /____ /____

I will think about all the things I am good at and what I'm grateful for in my day.

What are three positive attributes I have? I will say them out loud. "I am good at ..."

☺ My *Thoughts* for the Day ☺

I'm *thankful* for _____

I'm *thankful* for _____

I'm *thankful* for _____

DAY 30

Date: ____ / ____ / ____

Real success is loving myself and making good choices each day. It is being self-aware and creating my vision or purpose for my life.

What affirmations can I tell myself today? They always start with "I am" statements. I am kind. I am loving. I am beautiful.

☺ My *Thoughts* for the Day ☺

I'm *thankful* for _____

I'm *thankful* for _____

I'm *thankful* for _____

*"**Faith** - Free from expectation, faith takes me away from what I already have.*

I'm ready to leave past moments behind to make room for where I am.

I am ready to go where this presence takes me.

I will follow a path my head can't see, but my heart will show the way."

Justin Fuss

TESTIMONIALS

I have known Rita-anne for over 35 years and her passion for life is as invigorated today as it was when we first met. Rita-anne is capturing an important message of hope and self-reliance in her journal. Journaling has long been the pathway to find our inner self and in that finding we release our innate spirit on a pathway to a happier, richer and more satisfying life. We are the source of our own happiness and awakening to our thoughts and beliefs is a basic message of self-discovery. Rita-anne has lived a life on purpose and she delivers a message of encouragement. Explore her journal and discover your life-changing power and step into a life that you are longing to live. Visualize, Believe and Achieve... you are worth it.

Marie Soprovich BEd, Med, Founder & CEO Aquarian Networks Corp

I highly encourage you to journal in this book as you journey through life. You will be happy that you have written your thoughts, especially during difficult times. It will help keep you focused and realize that you are truly a gift from God.

Isabelle Zielinski B.A., B.Ed., Senior Sales Leader with Fifth Avenue Collection

Printed in Canada